Ha! Ha! Halloween

Ha! Ha! Halloween

By Michelle Medlock Adams

Illustrated by Meredith Johnson

ideals children's books™
Nashville, Tennessee

ISBN 0-8249-5508-0

Published by Ideals Children's Books
An imprint of Ideals Publications
A division of Guideposts
535 Metroplex Drive, Suite 250
Nashville, Tennessee 37211
www.idealsbooks.com

Color separations by Precision Color Graphics, Franklin, Wisconsin

Printed and bound in Italy by LEGO

Library of Congress Cataloging-in-Publication Data

Adams, Michelle Medlock.
  Ha! ha! Halloween / by Michelle Medlock Adams ; illustrated by Meredith
Johnson.
     p. cm.
  Summary: "A collection of quirky poems and illustrations that celebrate the
humorous side of Halloween, Ha! Ha! Halloween also features colorful tear-out
masks for children to wear. The book includes characters such as a pet werewolf
who uses the telephone, a monster who cleans rooms, and a goblin houseguest who
outstays his welcome"—Provided by publisher.
  ISBN 0-8249-5508-0 (alk. paper)
  1. Halloween—Juvenile poetry. 2. Children's poetry, American. I. Johnson,
Meredith, ill. II. Title.
  PS3601.D39H3 2005
  811'.6—dc22

                              2004028789

Designed by Eve DeCrie

10 9 8 7 6 5 4 3 2 1

To Mandy and Autumn.
You bring much joy and laughter into my life.
Love You "Aunt Missy" —M. A.

 For Elizabeth Reimer, my spoooooky pal! —M. J.

What kind of bat is best of all?
The kind of bat that hits a ball!

Knock, knock.
> Who's there?
> Ima.
> Ima who?
> Ima little hungry . . . bring on the candy!

EEK

Knock, knock.
> Who's there?
> Bee.
> Bee who?
> Be afraid—be very afraid.

Happy Hallowiener!

I have a dog named Maddie Ann.
She is the wiener type.

She celebrates each holiday.
She loves all of the hype.

So I decided to wish her
A happy Hallowiener!

She didn't like my little joke,
So now she's acting meaner.

She bit my leg. She bit my nose.
She's being really mean.

From now on, I'll wish Maddie Ann
A happy Halloween!

For Rent

Gently used costume—smells kind of sweaty—
Worn only once by my sister Betty.

I'll make you a deal. Just give me a call.
It's perfect for every Halloween ball!

For Sale

A witch's pot that's just like new—
Used once a year for making brew.
Please call me on the telephone
And leave a message at the tone.

Black Kitty

I have a cat.
He's black as night.

He gives some folks
An awful fright.

I don't know why.
He seems quite nice.

He won't eat you.
He just eats mice.

Wanted

A turbo-charged broomstick—
In bright red or blue—
It needs to have lights
And a sound system too!

Low mileage—a must—
And room for a cat—
I'd like an antenna
That's shaped like a bat.

If you have this broom,
Please give me a call—
Just leave me a message
On my crystal ball.

I Fell in Love with Dracula

I fell in love with Dracula.
I love that batty guy.
The first time he flew by my house,
He really caught my eye.

I think he's really, really cute!
We go out every night.
I have only one rule for him—
He's not allowed to bite!

Trick-or-Treat for Sauerkraut

This lady, who lives down the lane . . .
I think she's totally insane.

Every year at Halloween,
She does something that's really mean.
Instead of giving candy out,
She always gives us sauerkraut!

Pumpkin Face

I carved my pumpkin face tonight.
It's really quite a scary sight.

In fact, it scared my pet dog, Ted.
He's hiding underneath my bed.

A Monster Lives Beneath My Bed

A monster lives beneath my bed.
I swear that this is true.
I saw him just the other night.
He gobbled up my shoe.

And then he ate my dirty socks—
That makes me want to yack.
I wish that he would throw them up,
So I could have them back.

This monster seems quite harmless, though.
He never bothers me.
In fact, because he eats so much . . .
My room is now mess-free!

There's no more junk beneath my bed.
My mom is really glad.
This monster who's beneath my bed . . .
Is really not too bad.

Halloween Hayride

I love this time of year so much.
There's just so much to do!
This hayride sure is lots of fun!
It's great—ah, ah, ah CHOO—

Except for these (sniff) allergies.
I sneeze when I'm by hay.
But it's still fun. Ah choo! Ah choo!
It's just the price I pay.

Costume Ball

I'm going to the costume ball.
It's quite a big affair.
The guy I've liked for two whole months
Is going to be there!

I want this boy to notice me
And think that I'm a keeper.
Maybe my costume's not so bad—
I'll be a cute grim reaper.

Bobbing for Apples

Oh, yay! That time of year is here!
It's apple-bobbing time.
I love this time of year so much.
It's perfectly sublime!

I dip my head into the tub.
I try to bite the fruit.
I chomp and miss a hundred times.
It really is a hoot!

I may not get to bob this year—
I'm telling you the truth—
'Cause bobbing is quite difficult
When you're missing a tooth!

Take Me Out Trick-or-Treating

(To the tune of "Take Me Out to the Ballgame")

Take me out trick-or-treating.
Take me out there tonight.

Fill up my treat bag with lots of stuff.
I've got ten suckers, but that's not enough.

'Cause I want more candy in my bag.
Oh, please do not let me down!
Or I'll toilet paper your house
From the roof to the ground!

What Should I Be for Halloween?

What should I be for Halloween?
I just don't have a clue.
Last year I dressed up as a ghost,
And all night I said, "Boo!"

I think I'll be a regal queen—
That's what I'll be for Halloween—

Or maybe I will be a cat,
Or possibly a big, black bat.

Maybe I will be a horse,
But then I'd have to neigh, of course.

No, wait—I'll dress up like a teacher—
The scariest of any creature!

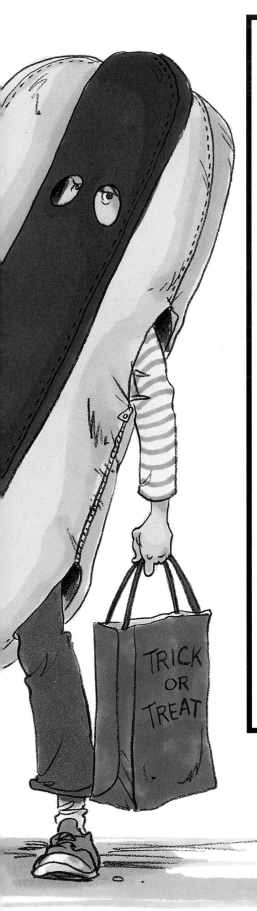

The Lame Costume

My mama made a lame costume.
I'll never ever leave my room.

She thinks it's cute. It's really not.
Still, it's the only one I've got.

Why couldn't she just buy me one?
'Cause then I could join in the fun.

Instead I'm doomed to be a nerd.
My costume looks really absurd.

My hot dog costume isn't neat.
Just who would want to dress like meat?

My life is ruined. I could die.
My friends will call me Weenie Guy.

I'm never gonna live this down.
I'm gonna have to move 'cross town.

I'm gonna have to change my name,
All because my costume's lame.

My Brother's Friends

My brother and his loser friends
Just had a movie night.
They rented every scary film
And gave me quite a fright.

I don't know which is scarier—
The movies or his friends.
I'd have to say his buddies 'cause . . .
At least each movie ends.

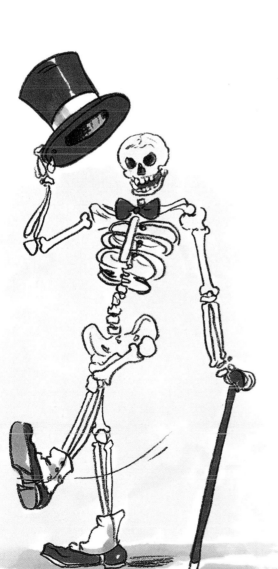

Dancing Bones

Dancing bones, dancing bones—
The skeletons all dance.
Dancing bones, dancing bones—
They dip and twist and prance.

Dancing bones, dancing bones—
All Hallow's Eve is here—
Dancing bones, dancing bones—
Their favorite time of year.

Dancing bones, dancing bones—
You won't be welcomed in—
Dancing bones, dancing bones—
'Cause you've still got your skin.

The Dreaded Hole

My trick-or-treat bag has a hole!
Most all my stuff is gone.
The lollipops and candy corn
Are on somebody's lawn!

I lost four packs of bubblegum.
And it was sour apple—yum!

I lost my cotton candy, too.
Just what am I supposed to do?

I found my favorite chocolate bar
Smashed in the road by someone's car.

I've got to salvage Halloween—
No matter what it takes.

I guess I'll steal my sister's bag.
I'm older—that's the breaks.

Pumpkin-Smasher

Beware! He lurks around the town,
This pumpkin-smasher guy.
He smashes pumpkins every night.
I really don't know why.

He smashed my pumpkin really good.
It's all over the place.
I think I'll bake a pumpkin pie
And smear it in his face.

Uncle Frankenstein

I love my Uncle Frankenstein,
But he's a little strange.
He's always been a tad-bit odd.
Mom says he'll never change.

His head is sort of big and square.
He's got bolts in his neck.
His skin is sort of grayish green.
He always looks a wreck.

I bet he's lived a million years.
He's really, really old.
And every time he shakes my hand,
He's clammy and he's cold.

My friends all call him "Scary Guy,"
But he's not mean at all.
In fact, this year I'm taking him
To my school's Costume Ball.

My Dog's Costume

I dressed my dog up like a cat
For Halloween this year.
But I don't think he liked it much.
He made that very clear.

He chewed up every shoe I own
And gave me dirty looks.
He growled at me an awful lot
And slobbered on my books.

I guess he's really, really mad.
He's acting really, really bad.

He doesn't want to be a cat.
I guess that is the end of that.

Mr. Monster

Mr. Monster is quite scary.
He is tall and very hairy.

Most boys and girls make fun of him.
This makes the monster feel so grim.

That's why he lives for Halloween—
A night when monsters are quite keen.

His "costume" always wins first prize.
The people can't believe their eyes.

"Your costume looks so real," they say.
He smiles and mumbles, "It's okay."

He trick-or-treats the whole night through.
It's his most favorite thing to do.

He wishes Halloween would last.
It always goes by way too fast.

So, if you see him out tonight,
Be nice to him . . . he doesn't bite.

He's really nice as monsters go—
The kindest monster that I know.

Flying Witches

The witches love to fly at night.
They race across the sky.
They laugh their creepy, shrieky laughs
As they go zipping by.

They race around the moon and back.
Their brooms are really fast!
I think I'll jump aboard a broom
The next time one goes past.

You see, I'd love to fly around—
Right through the starry night.
I'd swoop and dip and swirl and glide
And float just like a kite.

There's just one problem with my plan.
I'm sort of scared of heights.
I'm quite afraid of witches, too—
I know one, and she bites.

I guess I should forget my plan.
It's really quite insane.
I'll leave the witches' brooms alone
And fly inside a plane!

Counting Spiders

Some people count sheep when falling to sleep,
but sheep are too boring for me.

I count something fun, and when I am done
I'm sleepy as sleepy can be.

I like to count spiders—the ones that aren't biters!
So come on and count them with me!

One spider,
Two spiders,
Three spiders,
Four!
Big, black hairy spiders,
Let's count more!
Five spiders!
Six spiders!
Seven spiders!
Eight!
Spiders have eight legs.
Aren't they great?
Nine spiders!
Ten spiders!
Ten! Ten! Ten!
If you're not sleepy,
Then count 'em again!

Where Is My Werewolf?

Oh where, oh where has my werewolf gone?
Oh where, oh where can he be?
I miss my werewolf an awful lot.
He needs to be here with me.

But now my werewolf has run away.
He left me here all alone.
I hope that he calls me very soon.
I'm sitting here by the phone.

Although he's scary and kind of big,
My werewolf is very shy.
He's not the monster he seems to be.
He's really quite a nice guy.

So, if you see him, please send him home.
I need him here really bad.
He's such a wonderful furry friend—
The best one I ever had.

Halloween Stew

My homeroom teacher is quite strange.
She's weird as weird can get.
I know that she's an alien,
But I can't prove that yet.

Her favorite day is Halloween—
She loves that special date.
She says she's gonna make some stew
To help us celebrate.

I thought that sounded kind of nice—
To make our class some stew.
I thought, "That's really hip of her—
A real cool thing to do."

But then I saw her making it—
I thought I would be sick!
She threw in bellybutton fuzz
And toenail clippings—ick!

She served her stew to every kid—
That icky, stinky stew.
Of course, I didn't eat a bite
Because of what I knew.

I said, "No, thank you," to her stew,
And so she passed me by.
But then she said, "I've made dessert—
My special booger pie!"

Tombstone Funnies

Here lies Jack.
He sailed a boat.
Unfortunately, it didn't float.

Here lies Milly.
She was so silly.
She laughed and laughed and laughed some more.
She laughed herself right out the door.
She laughed herself right down the lane—
Too bad she didn't see the train.

Here lies Maggie Molly Mae.
She died of boredom, people say.
Her teacher really was a bore,
And poor Maggie could take no more.

Candy Corn Blues

I bought a bag of candy corn.
I ripped it open fast.
I munched on every single piece
Until I ate the last.

My stomach feels quite bloated now.
It's really, really big!
I think I overdid it 'cause
I look just like a pig.

I should've shared my candy corn.
Why did I eat it all?
I look like I just swallowed an
Enormous basketball.

Oh well. What's done is done, I guess.
I ate too much—it's true.
But don't give me a lecture, or
I'll yack all over you.

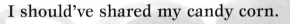

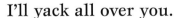

The Un-Halloween Party

The day is finally here, hooray!
Our party day at school.

The teachers give us party bags,
So that is really cool.

But we can't dress up anymore.
No costumes will be worn.

We do not mention Halloween,
Nor pass out candy corn.

The state has outlawed sugary stuff.
No candy is permitted.

And, so we'll munch on carrot sticks
And peaches that are pitted.

We will not mention Halloween.
We'll only talk of fall.

Forget the witches, ghosts, and bats.
Forget about it all!

No goblins, ghouls, or crystal balls,
And not one Frankenstein.

No mummies and no scary masks.
A pumpkin would be fine.

So party on, but party wise—
No booing anyone.

Celebrate "Un-Halloween."
It still should be, uh, . . . fun.

Toadstool Stew

"Have some toadstool stew," I said,
"And have some yummy cider.
I make them with a pinch of bat
And with a pinch of spider."

The witches come from all around
To eat my yummy stew.
They love my cooking very much.
I'm sure that you will, too!

A Goblin Came to Live with Me

A goblin came to live with me,
But I don't want him here.
He's messy, and he sort of stinks.
He's lived with me a year.

And trust me, that is way too long.
I wish he would move out.
He's angry and he yells a lot.
I wish he wouldn't shout.

There's only one thing left to do—
Do you know what it is?
I'll have to find another place
'Cause now my place is his.

Pumpkin Seeds

I ate some pumpkin seeds last night.
They tasted really yummy.
But now I wonder if I will
Grow pumpkins in my tummy.

Too Much Candy

We trick-or-treated all day long.
My candy bag is packed.
This evening I ate chocolate bars
Until I finally yacked.

I'll have to say, this holiday
Is really quite the bomb.
If only I could keep my treats
Far from my hungry mom.

A Ghost at the Door

There is a ghost at my front door.
I don't know what to do.
I'm kind of scared of ghosts, you see.
He might let out a "Boo!"

I don't think I could handle that.
I'd probably drop dead,
So I'll just act like I'm not home
And hide under my bed.

Pumpkin Thief

I bought a big, fat pumpkin—
The biggest one they had.
I scooped the insides out of it.
That gooey stuff smelled bad.

And then I carved a funny face
With a gigantic grin.
I carefully removed the top
And stuck a candle in.

That funny face began to glow.
It was a lovely sight.
I put it on our front porch steps.
It glowed and glowed all night.

But when the morning greeted me,
My pumpkin wasn't there.
Someone had stolen it away.
I yelled, "This isn't fair!"

I moped around for quite a while,
But then I found a note.
It said, "We took your pumpkin head."
And that was all they wrote!

I felt betrayed! I felt so hurt!
I wanted it returned!
The more and more I thought of it,
The more my anger burned.

I put up signs all over town.
I told my friends, "Beware!"
I even called the local cops,
And then I phoned the mayor.

My story made the local news.
The headline read: "Beware!"
They took a picture of my porch
Without a pumpkin there.

Most everyone seemed quite alarmed.
They all felt bad for me.
The mayor said, "Come to City Hall.
There's something you should see."

When I arrived at City Hall,
My mouth dropped to the ground,
For there sat my old pumpkin friend.
My pumpkin had been found!

The mayor said someone left it there.
It had another note.
The note read,
    "Here's your pumpkin back."
And that was all they wrote.

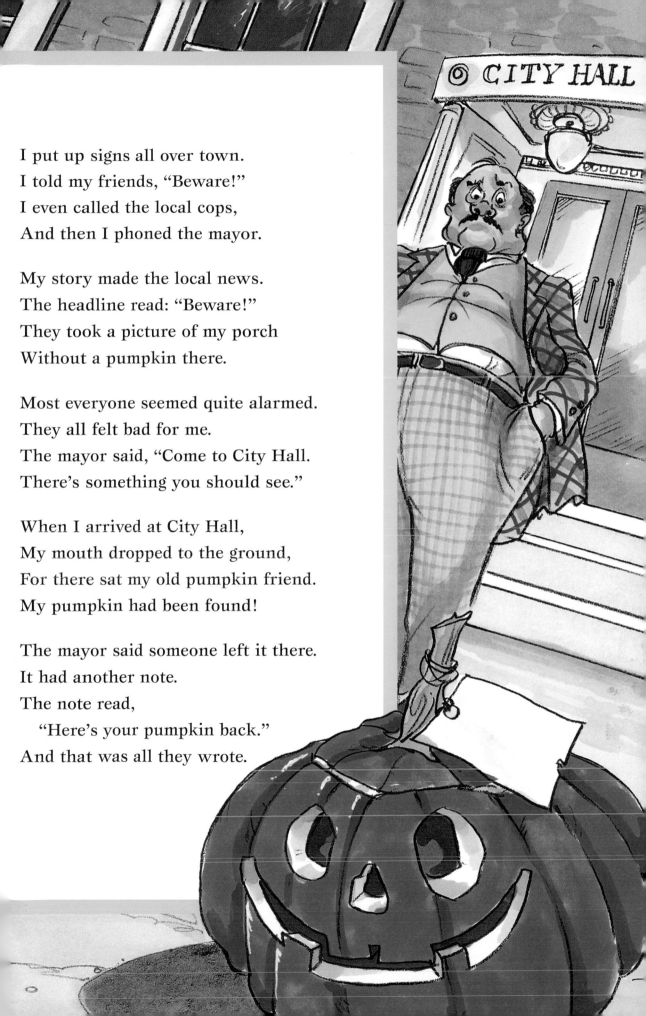

Trick Or Treat

Trick or treat.
Smell my feet.
Give me something good to eat.

Trick or treat.
We want candy.
Give us something really dandy.

Trick or treat.
Give us gum.
Hurry up and give us some!

Trick or treat.
Give us cake.
Not store-bought stuff, the kind you bake!

Treat or trick.
Make it quick!
We want to eat 'til we get sick.

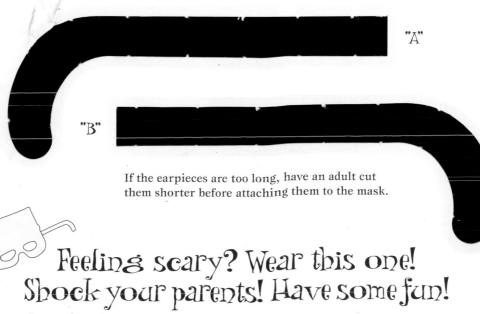

Tape earpiece "B" to this side.

Tape earpiece "A" to this side.

"A"

"B"

If the earpieces are too long, have an adult cut
them shorter before attaching them to the mask.

Feeling scary? Wear this one!
Shock your parents! Have some fun!